T0015281

This book belongs to:

....

WELBECK

Published in 2022 by Welbeck Children's Books,
an imprint of Welbeck Children's Limited, part of Welbeck Publishing Group.
Based in London and Sydney.
www.welbeckpublishing.com

Text, design and layout © Welbeck Children's Limited 2022
Illustration © Nic Jones 2022

Nic Jones has asserted her moral rights to be identified as the illustrator of this Work in accordance
with the Copyright Designs and Patents Act 1988.

Associate Publisher: Laura Knowles
Senior Editor: Jenni Lazell
Art Editor: Deborah Vickers
Designer: Anthony Hannant (LittleRedAnt)
Consultants: Dr. Julie Cosmidis
             Chris Tijani Barker
             Laura Buck

All rights reserved. No part of this publication may be reproduced, stored in a retrieval system, or
transmitted in any form or by any means, electronically, mechanical, photocopying, recording or
otherwise, without the prior permission of the copyright owners and the publishers.

ISBN 978-1-78312-849-5

Printed in Dongguan, China
10 9 8 7 6 5 4 3 2 1

EARTH CLOCK

THE HISTORY OF OUR PLANET IN 24 HOURS

TOM JACKSON

NiC JONES

TABLE OF EARTH

CONTENTS

CLOCK

INTRODUCTION

The Earth is never really still. It is always on the move, spinning on its axis once a day and moving around the Sun once a year. And it has been doing that for 4.5 billion years. Every second of every day, something is changing down on the surface. Every breaking wave wears away at a rocky cliff, a gust of wind blows a dust cloud into the sky, and the next rainstorm washes mud into a river.

At a much slower pace, the continents constantly shift their place on the globe and oceans shrink and swell, as volcanoes and earthquakes reshape the map of the world. Meanwhile, the millions of animals, plants, and other life that cover our planet are always gradually evolving into new forms, as they find new ways to survive. All these tiny changes, day after day, year after year, add up to make our amazing planet the place it is today – and has always been throughout its long history.

This book breaks down the long history of Earth into the 24 hours of a day. Every hour on the Earth Clock represents about 190 million years of natural history. Every minute is roughly three million years, and a second covers just over 50,000 years. By that timing, the first cave paintings are barely a second old and four seconds ago modern humans did not even exist. Rewinding the clock an hour and 20 minutes to 10:40 pm takes us to the Great Dying, a mysterious catastrophe where nearly all of life on Earth was wiped out. Going right back to the start, the Moon is about 13 minutes younger than the Earth, and for the first 45 minutes of its existence, our planet was a hot, dry rock with no seas or oceans at all.

Earth Clock takes you on a day trip through the many stages of Earth. Prepare to be amazed with every passing minute. It's time—let's go!

THE FORMATION OF EARTH

Our planet is built from the gas, ice, and dust that was left behindwhen the Sun formed and burst into light. The leftovers were swirling around the new star in a flat disk. All the planets, moons, asteroids, and comets in today's solar system grew out of this disk in a very slow process.

Earth weighs six billion trillion tons, and all that material grew from a tiny speck of dust. As the dust and grains of ice bashed together by chance, they began to cling together, growing into bigger and bigger lumps. The heavier lumps pulled the smaller ones toward them, growing ever bigger. All these impacts and collisions made the lumps of rock warm up, so as the young planet grew, it developed as a red-hot ball of liquid rock. After about 90 million years of this, the planet had swept up all the material around it. Earth was born.

Sun

Rocks

The area of the disk near to the Sun was made up of heavier materials like metals and rock crystals. Earth and the other rocky planets (Mercury, Venus, and Mars) formed in this region.

The Sun is a star made of a ball of hydrogen gas. The gas is being squeezed so tightly in the star's core that it gives out heat and light. This makes the star shine, lighting up Earth and the rest of the solar system.

Gas and ice

Further from the Sun, the disk was made from lighter material such as gas. It was also much colder out here, so those gases began to freeze into specks of ice. The planets that formed in this outer region are the gas giants, Jupiter and Saturn, and the ice giants Uranus and Neptune.

Gasses

Ice

Planetesimals

Planetesimals

In the early days of the solar system, as the dust and ice began to clump together there were thousands of small, rocky worlds called planetesimals. The planetesimals frequently smashed together, steadily growing bigger and bigger until eventually they had combined into Earth and the other planets.

THE MOON ARRIVES

When Earth formed, it was alone in space.
There was no Moon in the night sky.

One suggestion was that when Earth was very young and still soft rock, it was spinning so fast that it flung out blobs of red-hot liquid rock into space. Then these huge droplets of rock joined together to form the Moon. This seems unlikely because the Moon is so huge – a quarter of the size of Earth – which is far bigger than any other moon orbiting the other planets.

Another idea was that the Moon formed somewhere else and was captured by Earth's gravity as the two came very close to each other. If that were true then the Moon should be a lot like a mini-Earth, with a big metal core in the middle. However, the Moon is only one-sixth the weight of Earth, and that tells us that it is made mostly from lightweight rocks.

Moon rocks, brought back by astronauts who have visited the Moon, show us that it is made from the same rocks as Earth's mantle. The mantle is the thick layer of rocks under our planet's hard crust. This discovery suggested a new idea about how the Moon formed called the Giant Impact Hypothesis, or "Big Splash" for short. The idea says that in the first few million years of the Solar System, there were more than eight planets. It is suggested that around 4.5 billion years ago, a planet around the size of Mars smashed into Earth. The impact made both planets melt and merge together, and flung a lot of the planets' rocks into space, where they formed a ring of mini-moons. Over the next few million years, those rocks pulled themselves together until our big, rocky Moon had formed.

Thea

THE FORMATION OF THE MOON

The smaller planet is named Theia
after the Greek goddess who was
the mother of the Moon.

Earth

This impact theory also helps
explain why Earth's crust, its outer
layer of solid rock, is so thin compared
to other planets, such as Venus.

Orbital
debris

The Moon was much nearer to
Earth when it formed. To begin
with it was just 22,530 kilometres
away and has now drifted to
384,000 out. It is still moving away
at 1.5 inches a year!

Moon

A third of Earth's weight comes
from its iron core, but only a tiny
part of the Moon is made from metal.

THE FIRST OCEANS

Earth is an ocean planet. It is the only place in the solar system to have liquid water on the surface. These oceans formed once Earth had cooled down enough for it to form an atmosphere full of gases like steam, or water vapor. That steam then turned into clouds of raindrops, which fell to the ground forming first pools, then seas and vast oceans.

Before the oceans could form, Earth needed to go through some big changes. The young planet began as a seething ball of mixed-up materials containing metals, water, rocks, and gases. As Earth cooled, its mixed-up insides formed layers. The heaviest materials were the metals, like iron, which sunk to the middle of the planet. This formed Earth's core, which is still very hot today—almost as hot as the surface of the Sun.

The next layer is the mantle which is made from lighter material such as rocks. The mantle is still hot enough for the rocks to be melted into a thick liquid called magma. The next layer was the crust, made from a thin layer of cool, solid rock. The outermost layer was made from the lightest material of all – the gases. This created the first atmosphere, a layer of air around the planet.

Volcano

Water vapor and other gases escaped from the insides of the planet through volcanos to make the first atmosphere around Earth.

Crust

Mantle

Outer core

Inner core

Big tides

The ocean tides are caused by the pull of the Moon's gravity. When the first oceans formed, the Moon was much closer, and its pull of gravity was greater. In some places the tide would have been 195 feet high, four times that of the highest tides seen today.

Atmosphere

The first air on Earth was very different to how it is now. It was made from water vapor, carbon dioxide, ammonia, and methane. There was no oxygen, so anyone breathing this air today would choke to death in a few seconds.

The water vapor in the air cooled, forming thick rain clouds. As it began to rain, the water gathered in the hollow basins in the crust, forming the first seas.

Habitable zone

Earth is just the right distance from the Sun to be cool enough for steam to condense into water but not so cold that the ocean water freezes into ice very often. This means Earth is in the solar system's "Habitable Zone," meaning life can survive there. Life needs liquid water, and Earth is the only place where life is known to exist. However, the planet's first ocean was a completely lifeless place.

METEOR BOMBARDMENT

After Earth and the other planets had formed, there were still many millions of smaller objects spread out through the solar system. The ones made from metal and rocks are called asteroids, while chunks of space ice are called comets. Around 3.9 billion years ago, a big change in the position of the larger planets pushed the asteroids and comets out of position and they began to smash into Earth and the Moon.

The planet was hit by millions of space rocks, mostly quite small. However, about 20,000 of them left craters that were wider than 12 miles. The city of Portland, Oregon would fit inside a hole that big. A few of the impacts were much bigger than this, leaving a crater the size of Brazil or Australia. This part of Earth's history is called the Late Heavy Bombardment, and it probably turned the planet's surface back into a hot, dry ball of lava.

Water from space?

The comets that hit during the bombardment were mostly made from frozen water, which was added to Earth's own supply of water. Earth has a lot of water compared to other planets, and scientists have wondered if it all came here as comets hit the planet during the Late Heavy Bombardment. Space probes are being sent to collect water from comets out in space to find this out. So far, this space water seems to be quite different from the water on Earth.

Looking at the Moon

All of the craters left on Earth by the Late Heavy Bombardment have now been worn away by the wind, rain, and oceans. However, they are all still visible on the Moon. Scientists have figured out what happened on Earth during the bombardment by counting the lunar craters made at the time.

All the exploding impacts would have made the surface of Earth very hot. The oceans (or at least most of them) boiled away and large areas of the crust melted into lakes of lava.

Lava

15

PRIMORDIAL SOUP

Our planet is so full of life now, it is hard to imagine that when Earth was young, there was nothing living here at all. The best guess is that first life forms appeared in the oceans around 3.8 billion years ago, but it is possible that life could have appeared hundreds of millions of years before that. Our first clue that life had started are chemicals found in rocks of that age.

How did this life start? No one really knows the answer to that question. Today's living things all have a body made from cells (at least one). All kinds of cells are made from the same set of complex chemicals, things like proteins, sugars, and DNA. Living things make these chemicals inside their cells, but what happened before cells existed? Where did the chemicals of life come from in the beginning? One idea is that they were created by chance from a mixture of raw ingredients. That mixture is nicknamed the Primordial Soup. The best idea scientists have is that this chemical "soup" was "cooked" inside hot springs on the seabed, making simple life forms.

Seabed vents

The proper name for an undersea spring is a hydrothermal vent. Cold seawater soaks into the seabed, trickling through cracks until it gets so deep down that it starts to be warmed by the magma of the mantle. The water gets extremely hot but does not boil into steam. Instead, it surges up through other cracks and bursts out of the seabed in a jet of hot water. This jet often looks like a plume of dark smoke, and the vents are generally called "black smokers." This is because the heated water has collected a mixture of salts from underground rocks. As the hot vent water mixes with the cold, salty seawater, all those salts turn into specks of dust or crystals, which turns the water dark.

Chemical cookery

Many kinds of chemicals were being churned around inside the hot water of a hydrothermal vent, where they reacted with one another, sometimes breaking apart and sometimes joining together into larger more complicated substances. Over many millions of years, the chemicals used by life today were made by chance in these hot mixtures.

The first cell

The first life forms were chemicals, like DNA, that could make copies of themselves from raw ingredients in the Primordial Soup. These microscopic chemicals then surrounded themselves by a bag, or membrane. The bag protected the chemicals and held a supply of raw ingredients for making new chemicals when needed. This was the first cell, the first life on Earth.

LUCA

All life on Earth today—everything from an oak tree to a blue whale and a camel to a toadstool—is related to one single organism, or living thing. That organism is called LUCA, which is short for the Last Universal Common Ancestor.

LUCA was not the first organism that ever lived. Life may have evolved once or many times over, but all of today's life uses the same machineries for making proteins (the building blocks of cells) from DNA as LUCA. No one is sure when LUCA lived. The earliest fossils are bacteria that lived 3.46 billion years ago, so LUCA is at least a little older than that. For almost another two billion years, the only life on Earth were bacteria and archaea, two kinds of simple single-celled organisms that are about one-thousandth of a millimeter long. LUCA is thought to be an ancestor of both these life forms that lived in hot seawater filled with chemicals.

Long body

Scientists have compared the chemical system used by today's bacteria and similar simple life forms, and found that LUCA was probably most like the ones that had rod-shaped bodies and lived in places without oxygen. One of the closest relatives to LUCA are bacteria that live in our stomachs. Like them, LUCA may have had long, hairlike spikes called pilli that collected chemicals from the water.

Genes

Inside LUCA's cell, there was a bundle of DNA and small units called ribosomes. The DNA carried LUCA's genes: the instructions on how to build the cell from different chemicals. The ribosomes were the factories of the cell and followed the instructions from the genes to make the cell's chemicals. All cells alive today have DNA and ribosomes in them.

Extremophiles

LUCA is described as an extremophile, which means it thrived in conditions that would be too harsh for most of today's life. Chemical-eating extremophiles that live like LUCA are found in hot springs, deep inside thick ice and even in rocks far underground.

Chemical food

Early life did not eat other organisms. Instead, it got the energy it needed from chemicals in the water. LUCA is thought to have used chemicals such as hydrogen and carbon dioxide as its food, and as a result it produced methane. Methane is better known as natural gas and is used as a fuel. Today, methane is found in swampy and muddy places, but it was much more common when LUCA was around.

CONTINENTAL DRIFT BEGINS

When Earth got to about half the age it is now, its surface started to change shape. The land and oceans began to move in a process called continental drift.

Earth is the only planet in the solar system that has a solid rock surface that is constantly moving around. It works like this: the crust of Earth is not a single piece of rock like the shell around an egg. Instead, the crust is cracked into several sections, called plates. The plates are constantly moving at a very slow pace, because of movements occurring in the deeper rocky part of the Earth (the mantle). The bottom of the mantle is hot, while its surface is cool. The hot rocks, which are lighter, are pushing upward, while the cold rocks, which are cooler, are sinking down. This very slow swirling movement of the mantle, called convection, is causing the crust at the surface to break into plates.

In some places, rocks pushed against one another at the plate edges are melted into magma that rises to the surface and creates brand-new crust rocks. In other places two plates push against each other, and one crumples up on top of the other making tall mountains, while the other is pushed down into the mantle creating deep trenches.

Thick and thin

The crust that forms the seabed is very thin, in some places just a few thousand metres thick. This thin rock is made by volcanic eruptions on the seabed. The red-hot lava cools very quickly in the cold water and forms a dark and heavy rock. Areas of dry land are thicker parts of the crust, often around 30 miles thick. Although it is thick, the rock is lightweight, so it floats higher up on the mantle than the thin but heavy ocean crust.

For billions of years, continental drift has been rearranging the shape and size of the oceans and land, and even today the continents are all shifting a few centimeters a year.

Plates

Forming land

When the crust's plates push together, they create earthquakes and squash rocks together, which can make them melt and turn into magma, forming volcanoes.

Magma

THE GREAT OXYGENATION EVENT

Before 2.4 billion years ago, a short walk on the surface of Earth would be deadly. There was just no oxygen to breathe.

All the oxygen that is mixed into our air and water today was put there by plants and their relatives, such as microscopic algae and some bacteria. These organisms make their own food using a process called photosynthesis, which collects energy from sunlight and uses it to turn water and carbon dioxide gas into sugar. The waste from this process is oxygen gas, which is released into the air.

Photosynthetic bacteria had evolved long before this time, probably around 3.4 billion years ago. However, by about 2.4 billion years ago, there was so much oxygen being produced that it was changing the planet's atmosphere. Today, a fifth of the air is oxygen gas, and Earth's atmosphere is the only one in the Universe that has large amounts of oxygen in it. If astronomers ever find a planet orbiting a distant star with oxygen in its atmosphere, that may be a signal of potential life.

Stromatolites

These rocky bulges are stromatolites—some of the oldest fossils in the world. Stromatolites are formed by photosynthetic bacteria which grow together in sunlit seawater. As each layer of bacteria dies, a new one grows on top, and slowly, over many thousands of years, the stromatolite grows ever larger. The first stromatolites are 3.5 billion years old, and they would have been very common during the Great Oxygenation Event. There are a few rare ones still growing today.

Toxic air

The Great Oxygenation Event made it possible for life as we know it—including us humans—to live on Earth. However, it was a disaster for most of the older types of bacteria. The oxygen poisoned them, and today these oxygen-hating organisms only survive in rocks or mud where oxygen never reaches.

Carbon dioxide absorbed

Sunlight

Oxygen created

23

COMPLEX CELLS

Until 1.8 billion years ago, all life was tiny single-celled organisms like bacteria that lived in ocean water and on the seabed. Some kinds of these bacteria clustered together into balls and chains, where they could help each other out. However, there was nothing that looked anything like the cells in your body. These cells are much bigger and more complicated than the cell of a bacteria. This kind of cell evolved in an amazing way at this time.

The big idea is that our cells, and the cells used by all animals and plants, evolved when different types of bacteria teamed up to work together.

The cells of more complex life have many structures, called organelles, which work inside the cell. The organelles include the nucleus, where the DNA is kept very safe, and mitochondria, which supply the cell with energy. In plant cells there are also chloroplasts, which do all the work of photosynthesis. The chloroplast and mitochondria were once bacteria that somehow ended up living together to create a bigger, more complex kind of cell that could grow and combine to make anything from a giant squid to an apple tree.

Folded membrane

The first step was a bacterium cell growing a very folded membrane around itself. This might have helped it take in food or stick to surfaces, but later all those folds became a way of dividing up the inside of the cell. The DNA was wrapped up in a nucleus, and the cell had long tubes and chambers for making and organizing the chemicals it needed.

Mitochondria

Mitochondria

Nucleus

Folded membrane

A small bacterium enters the cell. Perhaps it was eaten by the bigger one? Maybe the smaller one was on the attack, or it was just looking for a safe place to live. We do not know, but whatever happened, the pair ended up living together as one unit. The new arrival used oxygen to release energy from sugars and other foods, and that gave the new cell a lot of energy to grow. Today those little power units are in every complex cell and are called mitochondria.

Chloroplasts

Chloroplasts

All animals evolved from the cell with just mitochondria inside, but plant cells also have chloroplasts. These were once photosynthetic bacteria that entered the cell and ended up staying.

25

SNOWBALL EARTH

At this time, the world went into deep freeze. The climate on Earth is always changing. Ever so gradually, over millions of years, the planet swings from being a warm place to being super cold. (The Earth is somewhere in the middle at the moment.) During the warm phase there is no ice anywhere on the surface, not even at the North and South Pole. The colder times are called ice ages, and thick sheets of ice spread out far from the poles.

Around 700 million years ago, the climate got so cold that ice covered almost the whole planet, creating the Snowball Earth. Our planet was frozen for at least 75 million years! The main trigger for Snowball Earth was probably that Earth's land was all bunched up at the Equator, where the weather is usually warm and wet. When warm rain falls on the land, the water reacts with the rocks and slowly breaks them down, and when this happens, carbon dioxide from the air becomes trapped in the rocks. As more and more carbon dioxide was removed from the air, it got colder and colder, because carbon dioxide is needed to keep the atmosphere warm.

We know this happened because rock features that can only be made by ice are seen at the Equator, which is one of the warmest parts of the planet. If there was ice here, then there would have been ice everywhere!

Open water

There were probably small seas of water in the ice near the Equator all year round. These got bigger in summer as some of the ice thawed out, and shrank again in winter. Life could only survive in the iced-over ocean and around hot, volcanic springs on land.

Pale planet

The white ice reflects sunlight and the Sun's heat back into space. More ice made the planet even colder, which added more ice, and so on. This link between color and cold helped make Snowball Earth last for so long.

During the day on Snowball Earth the average temperature was about –4°F (–20°C), which is normal for Antarctica today.

Snowball Earth finally thawed out because volcanoes added gases to the air that trapped the Sun's heat and warmed the world.

COMPLEX LIFE

The melting ice of the Snowball Earth left conditions perfect for life. The ice had ground down the rocks, adding minerals to the ocean. Meanwhile, algae and bacteria in the oceans had filled the air and water with plenty of oxygen. Bacteria and algae, plus many other kinds of life survive using a body made from just one cell. However, at this time more complicated organisms evolved, and they used millions—even billions—of cells that all worked together to make a body.

Today's animals and plants use billions of cells working together, but the first complex organisms are something of a mystery. They are called the Ediacaran Biota after the Ediacara Hills in Australia where they were first found 90 years ago, but the name is used for all life in the world during this period. No one really knows if the Ediacaran organisms are related to today's plants or animals. Some may even be entirely separate forms of life that have now become extinct.

Kimberella

Ernietta was a bell-shaped organism partially buried in the seabed. Its open end faced upward, perhaps to collect bits of food that sunk to the bottom. There may have been tentacles or some other mouthparts poking into the water that have not been fossilized.

Ernietta

Like many other members of the Ediacaran Biota, Kimberella had one line of symmetry running down the middle, with a "head" at one end. Tracks left as it crawled around the seabed look like its mouthparts were on the underside of its body and scraped food from the seabed.

Spriggina

Growing to about two inches long, Spriggina is thought to be a hunting creature. Its body had several overlapping segments with a larger segment at one end which is assumed to be the head.

Leaf-shaped Charnia lived in deep water, attached to the seabed. Although it looks like the frond of a fern or palm tree, it would have been too dark for Charnia to photosynthesise down here. The best guess is that Charnia filtered food from the water. It had no mouth so may have absorbed food straight through its skin.

Charniodiscus

Charnia

Swartpuntia

Swartpuntia was a tree-shaped organism which grew to about six inches tall and lived in shallow, sunlit water. It is possible that Swartpuntia could photosynthesise, and its fan shape helped it catch the Sun's rays from any direction.

Dickinsonia

The largest fossils of Dickinsonia are 4.5 feet across, and others are much tinier. The rounded creature is made from many segments fanning out from a central line running down the middle of the body from the largest section. It is thought that this section is the head. One suggestion is that Dickinsonia is an early form of placozoa, which are very simple animals that still live in the sea today.

29

THE CAMBRIAN EXPLOSION

This is the time that living things really took over planet Earth with an explosion of all different kinds of life. This process actually took at least 20 million years, but that is only a few seconds on the Earth Clock. By the end of this period, most branches of the animal kingdom we see today had appeared. That included animals like jellyfish, arthropods, and molluscs, as well as the first fish-like forms, which are our distant ancestors.

One big reason for the Cambrian Explosion was that animals evolved ways of making harder, stronger bodies. The Ediacaran organisms were most likely soft creatures that got squashed and injured easily. However, later animals were taking the minerals in the seawater to make hard shells, protective plates, and solid internal skeletons.

Another reason was the sheer power of biodiversity, or the variety of life. There were just so many new kinds of life by now, which drove the evolution of more and more types until the ancient oceans were teeming with life.

Pikaia

Wiwaxia

It might not look like it, but this small two-inch-long creature covered in spines might be related to bristleworms (a relative of earthworms) or molluscs. Scientists aren't quite sure.

Olenoides

Anomalocaris

Like most trilobites, Olenoides crawled on the seabed scavenging for food.

With its name meaning "strange shrimp," Anomalocaris was one of the first top predators of the Cambrian seas. It grew to about a half inch long, swam along with its blade-like body, and used its long, spiked mouthparts to grab prey.

Trilobites

Haikouichthys is the first known fish. It had a skeleton of bones inside the body and that included a spine or backbone. Every creature with a spine, from a shark and snake to an elephant and human, is related to Haikouichthys.

These sea creatures were a common sight in the Cambrian oceans. They have a body made from three sections or lobes, which is why they are called tri-lobe-ites. The topside was covered in interlocking plates that provided armour but also made the body very flexible. Some trilobites could roll into a ball. Trilobites had big eyes on the top of the head, and instead of using mouthparts to chew food, they ground up food by rubbing spiked sections of their legs together.

Marrella was a trilobite with a more graceful body so it could swim above the seabed. It used its feathery gills to help stay afloat.

Looking like a worm with long legs and a back covered in sharp spines, Hallucigenia is thought to be an early relative of today's insects and crustaceans, such as shrimps and crabs.

Marrella

Another hunter, Opabinia was much smaller than Anomalocaris, growing to just a few centimetres long. It used a trunk-like mouthpart to grab food from the sandy seabed.

Hallucigenia

Opabinia

With its domed shell and segmented legs, Canadaspis is thought to be related to crustaceans. Today's crustaceans include lobsters, shrimp and, on land, wood lice. It is likely that insects evolved later when a crustacean came out on to land.

Aysheaia

Canadaspis

A soft-bodied creature that resembles today's velvet worms, it is likely that Aysheaia is distantly related to Arthropods. No mouthparts are known for this animal, although it possibly fed on sponges.

LIFE IN THE SEA

As the oceans began to fill with more kinds of life, a frantic race began. Evolution drove the hunting animals to grow bigger and stronger and develop more powerful weapons for capturing their targets. In return, the prey also grew larger, so they could fight off attacks. As a result, animals grew steadily larger and more complicated—and they began to look a lot more like the animals we see around us today. By about 420 million years ago, the oceans were home to the ancestors of today's fish as well as the animals that live on land today.

Andreolepis

Most of the fish that live in the oceans today are related to this ancient species. It had very flexible fins made from flimsy rays of softer cartilage. Those fins were too weak for holding the fish's weight, but they were very good for swimming and steering in the water.

Early fish like Cephalaspis did not have a jawbone for biting or chewing on foods. Instead, this fish rummaged round in the sand on the seabed, sucking up worms and other food it found. At 19 inches long, Cephalaspis was one of the biggest fish around. It had bone plates on its head to protect it from attack from above.

This strange creature is one of the few that has survived to this day. Despite its name, this creature is not a crab. Instead, it is a distant relative of spiders and scorpions. It scurries across the seabed on its ten legs. It also has blue blood!

Birkenia

Cephalaspis

This small four-inch-long jawless fish scooped up soft mud from the seabed in its rounded mouth and filtered out any tiny fragments of food.

Horseshoe crab

32

Entelognathus

Entelognathus was a placoderm, one of the first kinds of fish with a jaw. Instead of having teeth, the fish's biting jaw was made from sharp bone that sliced and crushed its prey.

Orthocone

An early relative of octopuses and squids, this tentacled shellfish was the largest animal in the ocean at this time. Most orthocones were only an inch long but a few giants grew to 16 feet!

Pterygotus is a sea scorpion, a hunter that terrorised ancient oceans with its two powerful pincers. It belonged to the arthropods, a huge group of animals that includes today's insects, crabs, shrimp, and spiders. All these animals have legs made from hard plates that connect at many joints. The sea scorpions are now extinct, but they were very common in ancient seas. Pterygotus grew to nine feet long and was the most powerful hunter in the oceans.

Pterygotus

Prolepis (lobe finned)

Around this time, another kind of fish appeared. Its rounded fins were stiffened by strong bones. That made them strong enough to walk on the seabed and on the shore. These lobe-finned fishes were the ancestors of today's large land animals like frogs, lizards, mammals, and birds.

Hagfish

The slimy hagfish evolved around this time and is one of the few jawless fish that still lives today.

LIFE ON LAND

It is likely that the first living things to leave the oceans and move onto land were sea scorpions. They were doing this as far back as 430 million years ago, probably scuttling up the beach to escape a predator in the water. But they could not stay for long—and there was nothing else alive up there anyway.

It was not until plants evolved to survive in air that a community of animals followed them to live permanently on the land. These first land plants were much smaller than the ones we see today, but they still created a tiny jungle for all kinds of animal life, including the first insects.

Rhynia

This plant had a tube running up the middle of its stem for water to flow up the plant. This allowed it to grow taller and catch more light.

Cooksonia

This early plant did not have leaves or roots. It photosynthesised using its green stem instead. There was a capsule at the top of each stem which spread spores in the wind. The spores settled to the ground and sprouted into a new plant.

Trigonotarbid

Measuring just under an inch, Trigonotarbid was one of the first land animals. It breathed air and had eight legs. It was a relative of sea scorpions and horseshoe crabs, and was an ancestor of today's arachnids, which include spiders and mites.

Horneophyton

The living relatives
of this plant are
called hornworts.

Prototaxites

As well as plants, fungi also grew over
the land at this time. There were the
tallest things around, reaching up
to eight metres in some places. It
is likely that microscopic algae
were living inside these trunk-like
structures. The fungus gave the
algae a place to live, and the
algae provided the fungus
with food in return.

Aglaophyton

Aglaophyton is thought to be an early form of
a group of plants called clubmosses. Clubmosses
would go on to become enormous forest trees, but
at this time they are small and rare plants.

Nothia spread by growing its
roots sideways so new plants
can sprout in empty areas.

Nothia

This crustacean lived in pools and ponds and
climbed up plant stems into the air. It is
thought that the first insects evolved
from something like Lepidocarus.

Lepidocarus

Eoarthropleura

This early arachnid
was able to spin silk
like today's spiders.

Palaeocharinus

This is a relative of today's millipedes
and centipedes. At about half an inch
long, Eoarthropleura was one of the
biggest animals around.

THE FIRST FORESTS

At this time, the planet had become warmer and wetter, and plant life on Earth had evolved into something more like what we see today, with the first lush forests filled with immense trees. However, the tall plants were not related to today's trees. They were actually relatives of ferns and clubmosses.

The swampy forests they created were filled with life, including early tetrapods, or animals with four legs. Back then they were amphibians—animals that spent their early life in water and then lived on land as adults. Today, amphibians are mostly frogs and newts, which look rather different to their ancient ancestors. But all four-limbed animals—reptiles, birds, and mammals— evolved from these early tetrapods.

Griffinfly

Lepospondyl

This amphibian used its wide head to help it swim. The wide arrow-shape worked like a wing pushing the animal up to the surface as it moved through the water.

Pulmonoscorpius

The first air-breathing scorpion was almost identical to the scorpions alive today.

This dragonfly had a wingspan of two feet, which makes it about the size of a pigeon! No insect this big could survive on Earth today, as there is less oxygen in the air. The extra oxygen during the days of the first forests made it possible for the animals to grow much larger.

Tree ferns

These trees grew no flowers and made no fruits. However, they were the first plants to use wood to strengthen their bodies so they could grow to 164 feet in height. When the trees died and fell to the forest floor, there was nothing that could eat the dead wood. Today, the wood is devoured by insects like termites and beetle grubs and rotted away by fungus. Back then, the tree trunks covered the ground until they became buried under more trees and dirt. All this buried wood gradually transformed into coal, creating thick seams that fill rocks around this age.

Balanerpeton

This 19-inch-long tetrapod had the strong tail of a newt and the large, gulping head of a frog, but the wide outstretched legs of a lizard show us it spent its time mostly on dry land. There were many tetrapods around like this at the time, but Balanerpeton was not a direct ancestor of today's large land animals.

This big tetrapod grew to around five feet long, but its head was huge—making up about a third of the body. A body shape like this would be hard to haul around on land. Instead, Capetus probably lived in shallow water just next to the bank and moved back and forth between land and river.

Capetus

Arthropleura

Arthropleura is the largest arthropod that ever walked the Earth. And with more than 100 legs, it did a lot of walking as it grazed on the smaller ferns and mosses that filled the forest floor. The arthropods are a vast group of animals that include any animal with highly jointed legs and an exoskeleton, which includes today's spiders, insects, and crustaceans. Arthropleura was probably a giant relative of the millipede.

37

ON DRY LAND

By now, the world was warming up and the land had become much drier. The forests shrank and deserts grew.

The first large land animals used the same survival system as today's amphibians, such as frogs and newts. They had soft, damp skin and produced jelly-covered eggs, or spawn, that needed to be laid in water or buried in mud or damp soil. These animals could not live without a good supply of water, or their eggs would dry up and die.

As the world began to heat up and dry out, a new kind of animal evolved that could survive far away from water. They had skin covered in waxy, waterproof scales so they could withstand hot and dry conditions. They also laid eggs protected by a hard shell. The shell held a supply of water and food inside for the growing baby but still let air in and out so it could breathe.

These tough animals were the first reptiles. They are the ancestors of today's lizards, turtles, crocodiles, and snakes. Some also evolved into dinosaurs and then birds, while other early reptiles began to develop hairy skin and became mammals.

Pelycosaur

One of the first big hunters of the reptile world, Pelycosaurs had long pointed teeth and snatched fish from rivers and ambushed smaller reptiles on land. They had a sail-like crest on their back made from long spines that stuck out from their backbone. Pelycosaurs could raise and lower this sail and perhaps used it to show off to mates and startle prey. However, the sail's main job was to control Pelycosaur's body temperature. On a cold morning, the reptile hoisted its sail to catch the warming rays of sunshine. In the middle of a hot day, it held the crest in the breeze to get rid of unwanted heat.

38

Therapsid

This armored monster had thick skin and bony lumps on its face, and strong legs that held the animal's body high off the ground. Scutosaurus may have been a herd animal that traveled long distances looking for plants to eat in dry desert areas.

Scutosaurus

The big skull and long fangs tell us that this therapsid was a hunter, and its lean body and long legs suggest it was a fast runner, much like today's lions or wolves. There was not much around that could fight off an attack from a pack of these beasts!

Youngina

This small creature is a link between the reptiles and amphibians. It had a lizard's body with strong legs and a sturdy tail, and walked over land by wriggling its body from side to side, like lizards do today. Youngina is thought to have lived in burrows. It had a triangular head with small teeth and probably ate small insects.

Diictodon

These little animals had a big head with a beak-like mouth and small tusks poking out either side of the chin. It is thought that Diictodon ate roots and was a burrowing animal, digging its way through the ground with its mouth.

THE GREAT DYING

This is the most dangerous moment for life on Earth at any point in the history of the planet. The scientific name for the event is the Permian-Triassic Mass Extinction, but it is better known as the Great Dying. In the oceans, 96 percent of all species became extinct, including all the trilobites. This event was also the first and only time insects suffered the effects of a mass extinction.

Why did this happen? The Great Dying was likely caused by the gargantuan volcanic eruptions of the Siberian Traps, a large area of lava that formed in what is now Russia. This eruption was not out of volcanic craters. Instead, the lava surged out of long cracks in Earth's crust, and kept on coming out for about 11,000 years! In that time, 2.4 million square miles of lava (that's enough to completely fill the Mediterranean Sea) spread over the land, forming thick layers of new rock, called traps.

The eruption released vast amounts of carbon dioxide and other gases into the air, which made the planet warm up very quickly. Scientists estimate that the oceans near the Equator reached 40°C, which is the temperature of a hot bath. Not only did the heat kill many plants and animals, it also changed the chemicals in the water, making it impossible for other life to survive there.

However, life did go on. About eight million years later, Earth's wildlife was thriving again, and new kinds of plants and animals evolved, including the dinosaurs.

DINOSAURS

At this point in Earth's story, a new kind of animal began to take over the world. They were the dinosaurs—a name that means "terrible lizards"—and over the next 150 million years they evolved into the biggest and fiercest animals around. At this time, the seven continents we see today were joined together into a huge landmass called Pangaea, covered in forests and swamps. This was ideal for the dinosaurs, as they were able to spread easily and take over the world.

Postosuchus

In the early days of the dinosaurs, there were still bigger, meaner reptiles around. One of the biggest was Postosuchus. This predator was more closely related to crocodiles than dinosaurs, stalking its prey on its hind legs.

Placerias

Placerias was an early relative of modern day mammals, growing to impressive sizes.

Even though the dinosaurs were taking over, there was another new kind of animal evolving. The cynodont were small reptiles with sharp teeth, whiskers, and maybe a coat of fur. These little cat-sized cynodonts were the relatives of mammals, which include us!

Cynodont

42

One of the first flying reptiles, the pterosaur (meaning "winged lizard") had wings made of smooth skin that was stretched over its long arm and finger bones, like a bat. It was probably better at gliding than flying and used its wings to travel between the treetops.

Pterosaur

Plateosaurus was an early example of a giant dinosaur. It ate leaves and twigs and stood up on its back legs to reach up tall plants. It probably lived in herds to keep it safe from Postosuchus.

Plateosaurus

Tawa

Named after the sun god of the Hopi people of what is now New Mexico, Tawa is one of the earliest dinosaurs of all. It showed the big advantage dinosaurs had over other reptiles around at the time: it could walk and run on its large back legs and use its front legs as arms and hands for grabbing food.

Coelophysis was one fast-running hunter. It had a slender body with lightweight bones and a long neck for grabbing prey with its big, toothy mouth. Fossil experts think it preyed on smaller dinosaurs and little relatives of crocodiles.

Coelophysis

OCEAN GIANTS

At this time, the world's land was dividing into two separate supercontinents: Laurasia in the north and Gondwana in the south. A new ocean, called the Tethys, formed to fill in the widening gap between the two landmasses. Many new areas of shallow sea appeared along the coast and around islands, creating a lot of new spaces for ocean life. On land the dinosaurs were taking over, but the oceans were ruled by very different types of giant reptiles—plus some very big fish!

With fins and flat tail, the icthyosaur's body shape was ideal for swimming. At first glance, these animals look a lot like a dolphin or a shark, but they are in fact a kind of reptile. (Their scientific name means "fish lizard.") These reptiles breathed air at the surface but hunted underwater. Their long snouts were filled with small teeth for grabbing hold of slippery prey. Most icthyosaurs were about 10 feet long but the biggest were 65 feet. To see in deep, dark water, icthyosaurs had huge football-sized eyes—the biggest of any animal ever.

Icthyosaur

Cryptoclidus

Hybodus

Cryptoclidus *was another marine reptile, known as a plesiosaur. It had a long, rigid neck with a small head. Some think the long neck helped keep the rest of its body hidden in the murky waters, while its head sneaked into a school of fish or squid.*

This ocean-going hunter was a relative of today's crocodiles. It lived far out to sea and had a fish-like tail and webbed flippers instead of feet. Unlike crocodiles, Metriorhynchus and its kind were probably unable to return to land, and likely gave birth at sea.

Metriorhynchus

Named after the city in England where its fossils were first found, Leedsichthys was the biggest fish that ever lived on Earth. It grew to 52 feet long, which is the same size as a humpback whale. This monstrous fish was not a fierce hunter. Instead, it swam along with its mouth open, filtering out the tiny creatures called plankton that live in seawater.

Leedsichthys

Liopleurodon was another type of plesiosaur, from a group with short necks and huge skulls. At 19 feet in length, it likely tackled pretty big prey, which it stalked with four powerful flippers.

Liopleurodon

These were the main kinds of sharks around at this time. They had two types of teeth—flatter teeth that crushed shellfish, and sharper teeth to catch prey.

EARTH CLOCK
23:12
150 million years ago

GIANT DINOSAURS

The "Age of the Dinosaurs" lasted almost 200 million years and saw at least 1,000 different types of dinosaur evolve. By 150 million years ago the dinosaurs had become truly huge. Plant eaters evolved to eat vast quantities of leafy food, and predators had to get bigger and smarter to bring down these giant prey. This time also saw the evolution of a new branch of the dinosaur family tree. These amazing animals are still around today, only now we call them birds!

Few dinosaurs are as recognizable as Stegosaurus. This plant eater had flat, bony plates on its back. Their large and unusual shape suggests they mainly had a role in display, while huge tail spikes helped fend off predators.

Diplodocus

At up to 108 feet long, Diplodocus was one of the longest animals that ever lived. This plant eater used its long, slender teeth to strip leaves from the branches of trees.

Stegosaurus

Allosaurus

Allosaurus was one of the most common meat-eating dinosaurs of its time. Its skull was strong and well adapted to dealing with hunting, although its bite was a little weak. Serrated teeth helped inflict mortal wounds on its prey, whilst a pair of crests above the eyes acted as a display signal to others of its kind.

46

Brachiosaurus

While Diplodocus was longer, Brachiosaurus was twice as heavy, weighing in at 33 tons—as much as five elephants! Brachiosaurus was also very tall. Its long neck soared to a length of 40 feet, supported by the animal's huge and sturdy front legs. Like Diplodocus however, its skeleton was lightened by air sacs in the bones of the back and neck.

Archeopteryx

Plant eater Iguanodon was one of the first dinosaurs to be discovered by scientists. Its fossils were dug up in England in the 1820s. The animal was named Iguanodon because its teeth looked like giant copies of those of an iguana lizard. Iguanodons also had thumb spikes, which were powerful, straight claws on its front feet. These might have been used as weapons or for digging and gouging to get at food.

Iguanodon

Is it a bird or a dinosaur? The answer is something in between. Like a bird, Archeopteryx had feathered wings built for flight, but like a dinosaur it had a bony tail and teeth in its long beak. Archeopteryx lived separately from these other dinosaurs. It was a bit heavier than modern birds, so it probably climbed up trees using claws on its wings to grip, before jumping out into the air!

47

MASS EXTINCTION

In an instant, the world changed forever. An enormous space rock, at least six miles wide, smashed into a place called Chicxulub, on what is now the coast of Mexico. The impact created a hole in Earth's crust that was 12.5 miles deep and 93 miles wide—an area larger than the country of Wales. The sudden smash caused incredibly fierce rushing winds. The sea rushed into the crater and set off tsunamis that charged across the ocean. As these waves hit distant shorelines, the water loomed up to crests that were more than 3,200 feet high—that's higher than the tallest skyscraper in the world.

A cloud of superhot dust and gas blasted out in all directions covering an area 6,000 miles across. Anything living in the area would have been instantly vaporised, while those further away may have been affected by the scalding ash and debris that fell from the sky. The impact was at least a thousand times more powerful than the strongest earthquake ever recorded. Its shockwave cracked open the crust, causing part of the crust in that region to collapse, creating earthquakes all over the world. Clouds of dust and ash filled the sky and almost completely blocked out the sun for several years. Most of the world's plants died in the darkness, and its animals starved to death. Within a few years, 80 percent of Earth's life, including all the non-bird dinosaurs, pterosaurs, and most marine reptiles, were extinct. The survivors were all small animals, like mammals and birds, that were able to survive in cold temperatures.

Had the asteroid landed a little earlier or later in the day, it would have probably hit the deeper waters of the Atlantic or Pacific and not had such a massive impact. The dinosaurs were incredibly unlucky.

Tyrannosaurus rex and *Triceratops*

These two most famous of dinosaurs were there at the very end. The *T. rex* is the most famous hunting dinosaur of all. It had an enormously powerful bite, 12 times stronger than that of a polar bear. It is probable that *T. rex* killed its prey with a crushing bite to the neck. *Triceratops* defended itself from *T. rex* using a bony frill that stuck out from the back of the skull, creating a shield that protected the neck.

THE RISE OF MAMMALS

Earth has heated up a lot since the mass extinction that wiped out the dinosaurs and other large reptiles. There is no ice at the North and South Pole, and the areas of lush forests, swamps, and grasslands are much greater than they are today. There is plenty of room for mammals to evolve—and take over the world. Over the next few million years, the ancestors of all of today's main mammal groups, from aardvarks to zebras, evolved, but they were generally small and unlike the animals we know today.

This tiny tree-living mammal is an early relative of the primates, which include monkeys, apes, and humans. Teilhardina had big, forward-facing eyes like today's primates, which made it easier to see clearly in the jumble of forest branches.

Teilhardina

Phenacodus

Phenacodus *was the ancestor of a group of hoofed animals that have an odd-number of toes, such as horses, rhinoceroses, and pigs. It probably lived in small herds and ate plants.*

Oxyaena

This fierce-looking, 3.2-foot-long creature was one of the larger hunters around at this time. It had a sturdy jaw, filled with long, fang-like teeth. Oxyaena was an early member of the carnivore group of mammals, which now includes dogs, cats, bears, badgers, and seals.

Diplocynodon *was a fierce swamp hunter and an early ancestor of alligators and caimans. Today these big reptiles mostly live in the Americas, but they were once spread across the world. The crocodiles, such as* Diplocynodon, *had survived the mass extinction that wiped out other big reptiles, because they were so good at hunting along the water's edge—and still are!*

Diplocynodon

Trionyx

Trionyx *is a freshwater turtle with a difference. Instead of a tough protective bony shell, it has a soft shell covered in leathery skin. While hunting fish in the dark water clouded with mud it poked only its snorkel-like nose above the surface to breathe. This helped it stay out of sight from predators—but it did not always work!*

This big flightless bird was seven feet tall and equipped with an immense, hooked beak. It would be hard not to be terrified of this animal that patroled the forests of North America and Europe. However, experts think **Gastornis** *was a plant eater, not a hunter, and the beak was more likely used to slice through twigs and crack into fruits and nuts, not as a weapon.*

Gastornis

Diacodexis

This small mammal was only about 20 inches long but is thought to be an ancestor of today's even-toed hoofed animals, which include sheep, cows, deer, hippos, and giraffes. Like **Diacodexis,** *all these animals walk on the tips of their toes, and their thick hooves are the equivalent of our fingernails.*

AGE OF MONSTERS

The animals that took over from the dinosaurs were generally small. However, by now, 29 million years after the mass extinction, evolution has created some enormous animals by today's standards. The monsters were back!

Before big cats, bears, and dogs took over as the top predators on land, the biggest and meanest members of the carnivore group of mammals were creatures such as Hyaenodon. At about the same size as a lion, Hyaenodon had a good balance between strength and speed.

Hyaenodon

Andrewsarchus

The only record we have of this monster is a piece of its skull and upper jaw. From this, fossil experts can see that Andrewsarchus was possibly related to hippos and whales and was itself a huge 18-foot-long predator. It is thought it looked somewhat like a wolf with a long slender snout.

This monster was an early kind of brontothere, a name meaning "thunder beast." It was the largest herd animal around at this time, growing to eight feet tall and weighing eight tons. It had a gigantic 27.5-inch-long bone spur that grew from its skull creating a big bulging snout. It used this huge honker to make loud roaring noises. Embolotherium was related to today's pigs, horses, and rhinos.

Embolotherium

Urtinotherium

Urtinotherium was a long-gone relative of today's rhinoceros. It was one of the largest land mammals to ever walk the Earth, weighing in at about three times as much as an African elephant. Urtinotherium was more than 13 feet from its massive hoof to its immense shoulder, and its head and long neck could reach up even higher to nibble on the freshest leaves.

With nicknames like "hell hog" and "terminator pig," Entelodon was a scavenger and plant eater that lived in the forests of North America. Despite looking a lot like a giant warthog, and growing to the same height as the average professional basketball player, Entelodons were in fact relatives of hippos and whales.

Entelodon

53

EARLY HUMANS

The world has been slowly but steadily cooling for several million years. As more of the world's water freezes into ice around the North and South Poles, the sea levels drop and the rest of the world's land becomes drier. The lush jungles begin to shrink, and in their place grow hot and dry grasslands.

A jungle is home to many kinds of animal that are experts at living among the trees. One group are the primates, such as monkeys and apes, which have quick-thinking brains, good memories, and agile bodies. About seven to eight million years ago, one of the larger African apes, also an ancient relative of today's chimpanzees, gradually left the forest and evolved to live out in the open. Among this group of apes were our ancestors, and over time several different groups of human relatives lived in Africa's grasslands.

Homo habilis

Homo habilis, *meaning "handy human," was so called because this small relative was the first early human to be found with tools, although we now know other early human species also used tools. These tools included the chopper, which is a stone that is rounded at one end and cut into a sharp point at the other.*

Australopithecus

There were several types of Australopithecus, and they were the ancestors of all human species, including us. They were quite small-bodied apes, about four feet tall for one species. They walked on their back legs but still had long arms for climbing in trees, where they slept for safety from predators. Australopithecus lived along the edge of forests and in small woodland out on the savannah. They made simple tools for digging and cutting.

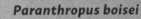

Homo erectus

This early human is probably the same species as Homo ergaster, but it was found outside of Africa, as far away as Georgia and China to Southeast Asia. Homo erectus means "upright human."

Deinotherium

Paranthropus boisei

Early human species had to watch out for Deinotherium. This was the largest elephant species that ever lived, being about a third bigger than today's African elephants. It used its downward curved tusks to rip bark from trees when there was no other food around.

This species was a heavily built species compared to other early humans. It was about five feet tall and weighed about 80 pounds. That size, along with huge teeth and jaw muscles for chewing, suggests Paranthropus boisei ate a vegetarian diet of seeds and roots.

Homo ergaster

This early human was about the same size as modern humans, and it is thought to have been the first human species to be mostly naked with only short body hairs. This would have made it easier to keep cool as it walked long distances over grasslands in the hot sun.

MODERN HUMANS

The modern human species, called *Homo sapiens,* meaning "wise human," appeared in Africa about 300,000 years ago. It probably evolved from *Homo ergaster,* or something very similar. Soon, *Homo sapiens* was the only human species in Africa, and around 70,000 years ago, it started to spread across Europe and Asia, where there were still other types of human living.

Cave art

A relative of today's rhinoceros, the woolly rhino lived alongside early human communities.

Around 45,000 years ago, early modern humans started to leave beautiful paintings and artworks in deep caves. They used charcoal to draw on the cave walls. They also crushed rocks and mixed this powder with water and blood to produce colored paints. Many prehistoric cave paintings show animals, and a few show scenes of hunting. Perhaps the pictures recorded a successful hunt, or perhaps they were drawn to bring luck for the next hunt.

The cave lion lived across Europe and Asia until 13,000 years ago. They may have been hunted for their pelts.

Social groups

Our ancient ancestors probably lived in small groups, occasionally coming together with larger numbers of about 150 people. We needed social groups of this size to depend on in times of difficulty, such as when food was scarce or ruined by scavengers.

Some primates, like chimpanzees, spend a large part of each day grooming other members of their group. This helps them stay friends. But a human group is too big to groom everyone. Instead, we learned to use language, so we could exchange news, make plans — and tell stories!

Gigantic woolly mammoths were still living in the Arctic region 4,000 years ago. The Pyramids of Egypt were already 500 years old by this time!

Other humans

Homo sapiens spread into Europe around this time and they found another species of human was already there... Neanderthals, named after the valley in Germany where they were first discovered, lived in Europe before and during the Ice Age and were bigger and stronger than modern humans. The two groups overlapped and about two percent of the genes of non-sub-Saharan African people today come from Neanderthal ancestors.

Modern humans would have also met the Denisovans, who were most closely related to the Neanderthals. The last Denisovans probably lived in New Guinea until around 15,000 years ago.

WHERE ARE WE NOW?

Human activity has transformed the face of the planet in just a few centuries. We have cleared forests to make way for fields, drained swamps to make space for our cities, and spread different non-native animals around the world. In more recent years, humans have started to make an even bigger impact on the planet through pollution and climate change. This moment in time equates to the final tick of the Earth clock. What happens next is up to us . . .

Humans everywhere

Humans are one of Earth's great success stories. More and more of us are enjoying a long and healthy life, and the number of people in the world has been going up and up for several hundred years. There are now more than eight billion of us. But we need to think about how Earth can provide us all a home, as we share this planet with millions of other species that are swiftly running out of space to live. Many creatures are forced to adapt by finding a way to live alongside us in our towns and cities, or run the risk of becoming extinct.

Plastic fantastic

Plastic is an amazing material. Most of it is made from the chemicals in crude oil and it can be used for a huge number of jobs, making everything from bottles to boats. However, unlike natural materials which decay and rot away, unwanted plastics just stay there. Plastic breaks apart into small particles and gets mixed into soil or ocean water. Eventually it will be buried deep down and become part of the new rocks forming in the crust. The rocks that form over the next few thousand years will have unique features that are only there because of what we humans are doing right now.

Climate change

Burning fuels and releasing other chemicals into the air is changing Earth's climate. The added gases, such as carbon dioxide, are trapping heat in the air, making the whole world warmer and creating more extreme weather. The chemicals in the air also mix into rain and eat away at rocks, washing them away faster than normal.

The warmer climate means that Earth is losing its ice around the North and South Poles. As the ice melts, extra water will be added to the oceans, making the sea level rise. A rise of just a few feet would be enough to flood many of the world's biggest cities.

A turning point

Scientists are warning that we humans are causing so much damage to the natural workings of Earth that the planet could suddenly transform into a much less hospitable place. Already we are seeing more extreme storms, frequent floods, long droughts, and huge wildfires. However, we already know how to fix these problems if we all work together. The question is—will we do it in time?

WHAT WILL TOMORROW BRING?

We can only guess at what Earth will be like in the far future. We know that a species generally lives for about one million years before it evolves into something else or becomes completely extinct. Our species is still very young, but we have already had a very big impact and are working to fix climate change and habitat destruction. What will those changes mean for the future of life on Earth?

The changing climate will force hundreds of millions of people to move to new places to live. As well as leaving places that have become too hot, people may move away from the ocean. Nearly half of the world's population lives within 60 miles of the sea, and rising sea levels and extreme storms will mean many oceanside cities will be flooded regularly. But this may force us to innovate, creating new technology using renewable energy sources to help us survive in inhospitable places.

An extreme climate may mean the end for many species, while others might evolve in all kinds of ways, potentially becoming unrecognizable from the animals we know today. For example, some rodents, like the house mouse and brown rat, have always done well living alongside humans. In the distant future, these rodents might evolve into fierce bear-like hunters or giant grazing beasts. Crabs are a successful species able to live in water and on land—already some species have left the water and live up trees in the jungle. Maybe Earth will become a planet of crabs?

If humans are able to tackle climate change in time, perhaps the temperatures, weather, and sea levels will not be so extreme—we may establish cities and a way of life that works with nature and allows wildlife space to thrive.

One day, perhaps in many millions of years from now, the human beings of today will become extinct. Perhaps we will die out like the dinosaurs or evolve into a new kind of human and find our way to distant planets. But whatever happens, the Earth will still be here—spinning on its axis in the darkness of space, surrounded by billions of stars. And the Earth clock will keep ticking.

TIMELINE

The life story of Earth is written in this chart, known as the geological timescale. The timescale includes all the major chapters in our planet's history, from its birth as a hot ball of liquid rock, to its many ice ages, mass extinctions, and explosions of life.

The timescale has been put together over many years of hard work by geologists. They use the fossils and rocks found underground as their timekeepers. Rocks—and the fossils inside them—found nearer the surface are always younger than the ones that formed deeper down.

As the Earth clock ticked away, there were many big, often sudden, changes. For example, very old rocks show when Earth had cooled into a rocky world, or when the oceans began to cover its surface. Much later the communities of wildlife that ruled over Earth went through many changes, often wiped out in huge extinctions. The timescale uses these big changes recorded in the rocks to mark out the different phases of Earth's history.

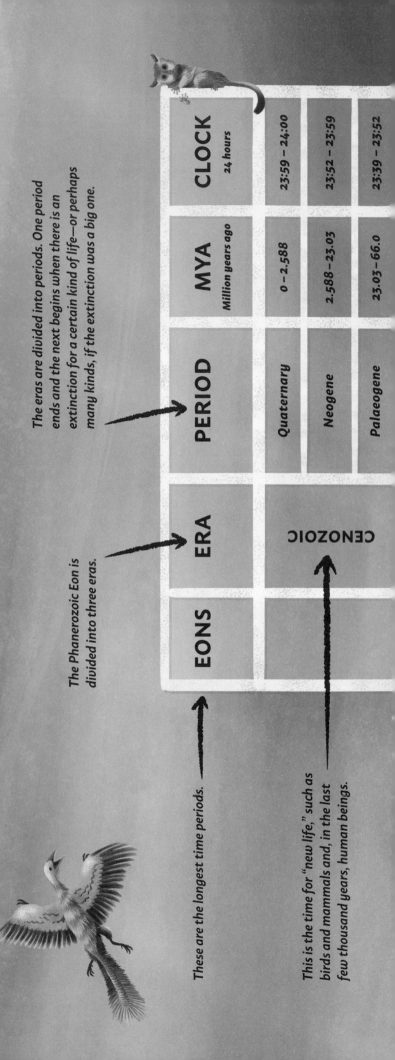

These are the longest time periods.

The Phanerozoic Eon is divided into three eras.

The eras are divided into periods. One period ends and the next begins when there is an extinction for a certain kind of life—or perhaps many kinds, if the extinction was a big one.

This is the time for "new life," such as birds and mammals and, in the last few thousand years, human beings.

EONS	ERA	PERIOD	MYA *Million years ago*	CLOCK 24 hours
	CENOZOIC	Quaternary	0 – 2.588	23:59 – 24:00
		Neogene	2.588 – 23.03	23:52 – 23:59
		Palaeogene	23.03 – 66.0	23:39 – 23:52

Eon	Era	Period	Millions of years ago	Time
PHANEROZOIC	MESOZOIC	Cretaceous	66.0 – 145.5	23:14 – 23:39
		Jurassic	145.5 – 201.8	22:56 – 23:14
		Triassic	201.8 – 252.17	22:40 – 22:56
	PALEOZOIC	Permian	252.17 – 298.9	22:25 – 22:40
		Carboniferous	298.9 – 358.9	22:06 – 22:25
		Devonian	358.9 – 419.2	21:47 – 22:06
		Silurian	419.2 – 443.4	21:39 – 21:47
		Ordovician	443.4 – 485.4	21:26 – 21:39
		Cambrian	485.4 – 541.0	21:08 – 21:26
PROTEROZOIC			541.0 – 2,500	10:47 – 21:08
ARCHAEN			2,500 – 4,000	02:51 – 10:47
HADEAN			4,000 – 4,500	00:00 – 02:51

MESOZOIC — This "middle life" section is the age of giant monsters and beasts that ends with the extinction of the dinosaurs and many other prehistoric creatures.

PHANEROZOIC — Earth is still in this eon today, which has seen the evolution of a huge variety of life.

PALEOZOIC — This name means "old life" and covers from the Cambrian Explosion to the Great Dying.

PROTEROZOIC — Oxygen begins to fill the air, and the first complex life evolves.

ARCHAEN — Earth's surface is now solid with huge oceans. The first life forms.

HADEAN — The young Earth is mostly covered in lakes of lava and is being bombarded by giant asteroids and comets.

INDEX

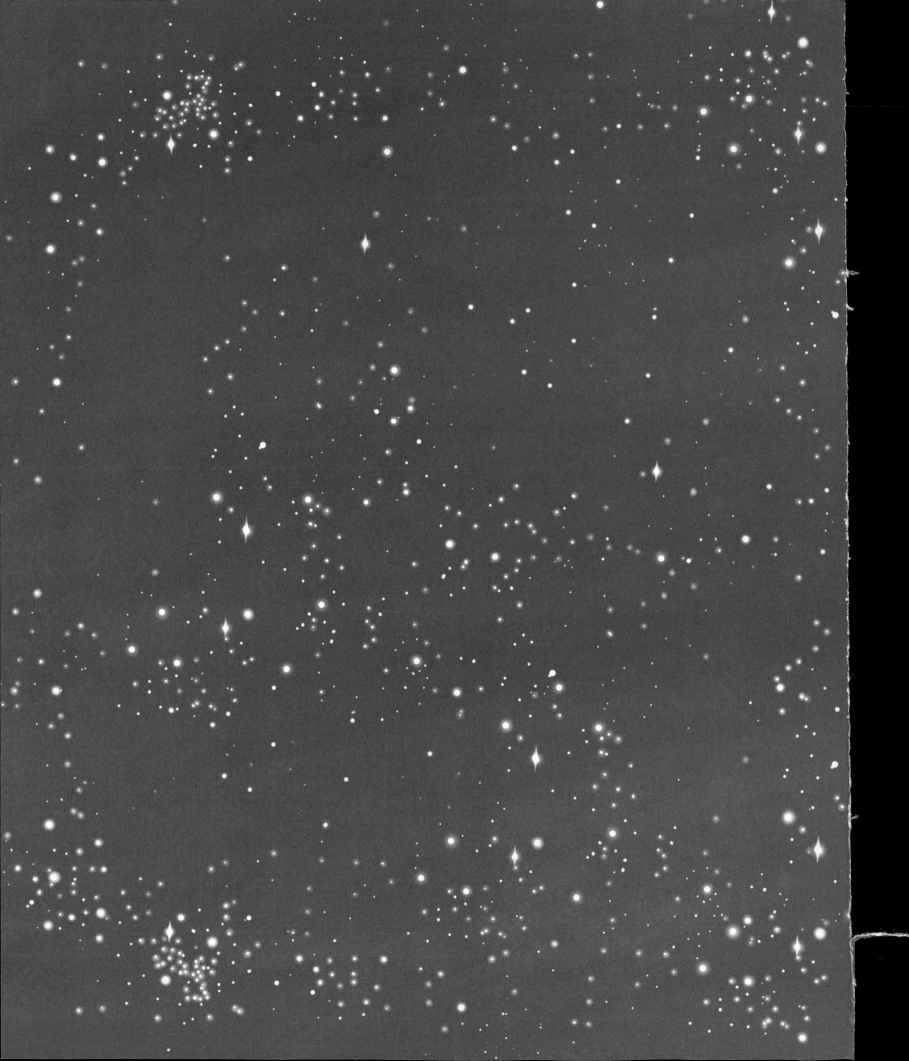